Badgers in a Time of Corona

Words, sketches and photographs

by

Thomas Gray

Published by Thomas Gray 2020

ISBN 978-1-716-56125-2

1

Thomas Gray (13) lives in rural Hampshire with his parents and two brothers. In addition to a keen interest in badgers, Thomas enjoys fishing, playing cricket, football, rugby and the violin. He attends Perins School (when it's open).

Thomas pictured below with a clump of Bird's Nest Orchids.

I dedicate this book to my friend Mike who has taught me so much about our local woods.

Thank you.

Thomas Gray

Introduction

When the lockdown started, it immediately meant that I could spend more time with the nearby badgers. The local sett, unknown to most, consisted of lengthy tunnels and large entrances that churned up the woodland slope inside out. The sheer size of some of the spoil heaps indicated that the animals had been here for quite a while, perhaps for decades, potentially more. I had gained the knowledge of the colony's whereabouts a few years ago, so I watched and monitored it frequently in my spare time. Now, watching them is a very pleasurable experience, but after reading a lot on the topic, I came to some articles where various different people had completely gained the badgers' trust. This could enable them to hand feed, stroke and hold the stripy creatures, right outside their sett.

As I said before, I had been visiting the sett for some years, so they will definitely have smelt me before, and in a way, acknowledge that I probably wasn't going to go away any time soon. This gave me a slight advantage if my "goal" was to make sure the badgers had properly acquainted themselves with my scent, but not a huge one. I do know however, that I am making some progress, as numerous times in the fading light, has the wind hastily changed towards an emerging badger. This would normally have been a catastrophe for their night, and mine as well, because these times are when the creatures are most jumpy and on their guard, but no, they did not seem to mind that I was there at all (these were recent occurrences though).

Trail cameras are considered cheating by many naturalists, but they are excellent for recording the wildlife of the owners' choice, and depending on where it is placed, the better quality the photo/video will be, so the word cheating is not applicable. Anyway, my point is that these devices have helped me considerably. For example, I have started putting clothes out by the entrances, and by training cameras on them, I can see how the badgers are reacting to my jumper or coat. By using this method, I am able to see if the animals are ready to be watched very closely, but please note that hand feeding them like dogs will likely take numerous months, slithering to years, to accomplish.

I would advise to place sticks in front of the active sett entrances to see where they are coming out from, along with on regularly used paths. It has worked well for me, monitoring their moves and observing if they are becoming bolder altogether. Using cameras and sticks are only optional, as the most important thing to do is to sit outside the holes at dusk. This will make sure that your scent will be hanging around in places the badgers will smell, and will eventually make the badgers feel comfortable in your presence.

Being completely honest though, I feel that the chances of badgers eating out of my hands are low, and I just appreciate being able to watch them at close quarters at all. I will try not to stop anointing the setts, but I do not expect anything big, as the thrill of one coming right out, a few feet away without myself detected, is equally exciting.

I hope that by reading this narrative journal, you will see badgers as different animals, and that hard work will eventually pay off.

Thomas Gray November 2020

The Badgers of Downton Grove

Adults: Cabbage, Husky, Pirate, Roman, Eilean, Freya and Frond
Cubs: Buckthorn, Cotton, Hornbeam, Rough, Scrub, Silvia, Siege, Stubble and Tumble.

The Badgers of Lockley Wood

Adults (cubs are un-named): Bramble, Hawthorn, Maple, Parvus, Ol' Doris and Stubbers.

April 2020

Getting started

16th April

As I normally would, I arrived in the wood and went to anoint the large sett close to where I was standing. (Anointing is leaving a piece of my clothing by the sett or sitting close by so the badgers get used to my scent). It was all quite normal – there had been some sticks pushed over in various entrances and no hard evidence of new cubs. Though when I had finished sitting in the large hole that burrowed under the old log pile, I heard muffled grunting, snorts and wheezes. I slowly walked over to the thicker logs, thinking it an injured rabbit. The racket seemed to be coming from an old hole I had forgotten about, although with nothing to be seen. But almost as I thought it was probably a large rat, a black and white snub nose came back and forth

from in and out the entrance! It could not have been more than 40 cm long from where I was standing, (which was about three feet away). As close as I was though, it did not seem to mind I was looming over it; the cub looked at me quite a few times. I did take a photo, but I knew this encounter would be brief, as coming out at about 5.20pm is rare behaviour so it was just an insignificant snap of its head. It turned out that it was a brief meeting, as when my younger brother shouted halfway across the wood, the youngling retreated into its extensive home.

17th April

I skirt the woods very frequently, and on a walk round the back of them (on my way to the sett), my eyes came upon a skulk of pink/purple flowers. Having been in the bluebell season where there are sheets of colour on the leafy floor, I immediately considered them the species I would expect them to be. Despite this, my curiosity got the better of me, and to my surprise, the petals were actually the spikes of Early Purple Orchids, one of three species of orchidaceae within these trees. This find may not have anything to do with badgers, but flowers like this are rare, and a sight is worth taking notes of.

18th – 22nd April

Springtime seems to be the more favourable season for rabbits, as they get increasingly diurnal throughout this time of year. Like badger cubs, the kits start emerging from their burrows in or after Easter, so unsurprisingly, I have spotted numbers of premature rabbits nibbling on grass close to the hidden entrances on the woodland boundary. They are often in the field as I go to put my cameras out, frolicking in the barley. Speaking of cameras, I made sure they overlooked the badger sett entrances, as well as my t–shirts on the spoil heaps. After leaving them out for three nights, I collected them to find that annoyingly,

they had taken bluebells in as bedding, through a hole behind where I was recording. I first thought that they had deliberately veered away from my scent, but there happened to be no footage of a badger poking its nose to smell my clothing. What is more, there was a very strong northern wind, and a badger could not possibly have detected my top from within its extensive home. I wasn't too pleased that I couldn't see how they reacted to my clothes, but I ended it with the sighting of six hare sprinting up and down the field like bunched Olympic runners, reminding me vaguely of the rabbits of *Watership Down* hurtling away from danger.

26th April

Because of the experiments I am doing on the sett nearby, I did not want to go badger watching there, as my 'scent marking' may have disrupted emergence, but that was unlikely. Fortunately, the area is mostly hilly woodland and field, so, as well as I had found every colony around, the job of discovering setts proved an easy task. Therefore, with so many of them in the vicinity, the choice of where to sit was not a hard one to make.

Downton Grove wood is long and thin, gradually thickening towards the west. The Watercress track slides alongside the trees, digging a V into the ground, adapting to the rather steep south – facing slope. The sett was first mentioned to me by a school boy on the bus, claiming to have seen badgers there before at night while strolling in his pyjamas (???), so I eventually went badger watching in this venue. I brought my Dad along with me, and we both agreed that the spoil heaps indicated decades and decades of age.

The light was still shining considerably as we sat down accordingly to the wind at around 8pm, on a very conveniently placed tree trunk a few inches off the ground. Not only this, but this viewing spot was pretty much on the public footpath giving us two helpful advantages: the animals living below us will have slowly adjusted to human smell, as well as being able to access the area. We were both hoping that nobody will spoil the evening by running by in headphones, but soon realised that there was little chance of that, since not many will be out during lockdown.

I was looking up and around me to know what my surroundings were, as I normally would; the entrance in front of us was active, but I was not expecting anything from there, as there were nine or 10 other, more used holes to our left. The furthest entrance, (about 30 feet away) had a spoil heap the size of a car. Half that distance, there was a sandy entrance with hardly any pushed out soil at all, but it was new, so my hopes were high.

A bird made a right old racket behind us, so I naturally looked, followed by my Dad excitedly whispered *Badger!* Hastily turning around, a conspicuous head bobbed up and down in that small entrance I mentioned earlier. Breaths held, we both watch it in eagerness, as it heaves its behind completely out of the tunnel. This badger looked like a yearling, for its undercoat was rough and 'jagged' but his hide was a beautiful silver, a different silver, a silver a professional artist would be immaculately proud of. Its head was a lovely shape, slightly curved with those impeccably striking black lines, snaking easily down to deathly black eyes that stare deeply into one's soul. This image of the creature was given to us many times, it frequently stopping to look at us, as it ambled off to our left, even closer this time, before, retiring back down to the same entrance in no hurry, leaving us both in a trance.

It was a few minutes before the second one came out of the same hole. This one was very big – he was bulky and stocky, with a wide, hooked nose. He too, did not properly keep an eye on the wind, and waddled out of its quarters, gazing at us from time to time. Even though we did not move one bit, their eyesight must have been poor, as they emerged in broad daylight. This badger did not have much to do, as he sat outside his home for a few minutes, and then waddled back in. Since it did it in a refined manner, we were optimistic for more emergence later.

Though not after five minutes! Once again, the yearling's head peered out from the exact same place, and heaved its rump out of hiding, looked at us, "then peered down, as if to say – what are you waiting for, its quite alright up here!" (Ernest Neal in *The Badger*). As if by magic, a smaller head appeared, but it turned out to be another, darker, smaller sow, with noticeably rounded ears. She didn't seem to take stuff for granted, and sat bolt upright, watching our every move (which wasn't much). The cub obviously couldn't be bothered to wait, and wandered off, still very much where we could see him, down the railway bank and somewhere else. Meanwhile, the sow was content with us being here, and came forward a little, then to the sycamores, closer still. After a slow walk around, she retreated down to the same hole – this is getting into a bit of a habit now! Sure enough, she came out very shortly afterwards, without testing the air at all this time. She quickly came out where she originally did, but decelerated her pace, as she sniffed for presumably grubs, staring at us, possibly becoming more uneasy with two unknown objects just there. Twice did she look at us in a few seconds, but even with the wind in our favour, and us not moving an inch, she still quickly ran down the hole.

I did not expect to see any more from her that evening, but there was still hope to see the large boar. Just as we guessed, he came plodding out shortly afterwards, and went to the sycamores to the left. He snaked through the shoots, and crossed the footpath, 10 feet away from where we sat, foraging in the closely packed earth for a few minutes, and didn't see us once, he was so busy. A rustle echoed from about 50 metres away to our left, making the badger stop still, only for him to jog – trot towards the noise. It was the last we saw of the three different badgers who emerged six times before our eyes in broad daylight, but it made me wonder. The sett itself was huge, with many intertwining tunnels that go on for ages, and it seemed unlikely that only three badgers could manage it so well. A theory is that because the cubs have undoubtedly been born, then at least one other one will be down there supervising them. Another large entrance is 50 metres to our left, as a part of the sett we were watching, so when the boar heard a rustle, it could have been another different badger.

That evening was lucky, since I have never seen badgers emerge in complete daylight, and even though there have been numerous blank nights on other setts, a dedicated watcher will

be even more determined to see what we saw – a simple, lumpish shape, but really, so complex in every detail, at close quarters, in the wild. I didn't take a camera, as I had no idea that the light would be so good, but now I know this, there is only one question that is constantly badgering my mind, and that is when shall I go again?

New Faces

May

2nd May

When anointing the sett, I had many times seen a leveret sitting around the brambles, munching on the close – set grass while sitting on the spoil heaps. I had numerous new photos of the rabbits, so after noticing it growing darker and lankier, I reckoned it would provide a great opportunity for photographing a brown hare. Stalking right up to to hare when it was devouring some new shoots, and it couldn't care less that I was a couple of yards away, gave me great confidence.

The next two nights were a kamikaze of easterly winds bringing down buckets of rain, putting me off from going to the setts, but the following day was rather sunny with a warm breeze. This happened to be one of the days, in which my family and another family rebelliously met up by the woodland edge. On the way back, the others veer left, while I go straight on towards the spoil heaps.

I stepped ever so quietly so as not to disturb my target. After a few minutes of peering about, I started to lose hope, so I began to do what I normally would. Walking more effortlessly now, I soon saw that white tail bob up and down out of the nettles in front of me, then bounding off behind some sticks in front. I could make out its ears moving slightly, so I got my camera lens cap off, which in doing so, lost me the sight of the hare. I walked cautiously towards where I thought it was, but it was nowhere in sight, but, oh yes! There was is again, only to

have its ears right down its back. I remember my Grandad telling me you could stalk right up to a tense hare, if you made little movement. I did the same.

I was taking photos at all angles, but I just was not close enough, so I carried on, all of this time finding the depth of field very difficult, as there were so many twigs in the way. I finally took the right photo when I was less than two metres away, appreciating how close you can get to nature, if you know where to look.

4th May

Due to a prolonged period of dank weather, I hadn't gone badger watching for a week, so I alone, walked to the same sett in which I took my Dad. My sights were set high, as I could still vividly remember my last experience, so decided to take a camera with me. Biking would have been quicker to get there, but I considered the light conditions after dark, so I simply walked round the meandering lanes towards the evening's destination.

Badgers are extremely nervous animals; therefore, I was concerned that the sound of a strange black thing coming to life would startle them. I took the precaution, and thought that I should turn it on a few minutes after I settled down, which turned out to be 7.44pm. Despite night time closing in, in three quarters of an hour, the air was actually warm, and slightly muggy, giving me the option to take my winter coat off. That, I did. The clock ticked past eight, so I turned my camera on, aiming to film them, rather than photograph them, as the click on the record button was much quieter.

I was put in a great mood when the small sow came out 10 minutes later. I just caught a bulky figure lumber along the gnawed, bashed and generally beaten up railway fence 30 feet away, excitedly recording at the same time. Unlike my last viewing, she did not stick around for long, and was foraging her way up the track, eventually disappearing from my sight, and the lens's. Complete darkness was in an hour, and the sunset half that time, showing that the badgers in this colony emerge frequently in daylight, so I knew I was in a vantage point from where I sat.

Almost immediately, did I see another badger scratching behind their ear in the same place where the first one emerged. Unfortunately, I soon lost sight of it shuffling between the bushes; it probably went down to the railway tracks and back up. So far, the hosts seemed to be coming out of the entrances situated on the grassy bank, still very close, but out of sight. I admit, I was slightly disappointed that I may not be able to see one poke its nose out of the tunnel, though, these thoughts were heartened by the fact that it was very likely one would come close to where I was sitting.

As if by magic, an iconic head popped right up, from the entrance with a minute spoil heap! I immediately recognised it as the boar with the snubbed, knobbly nose – the third to emerge tonight, considerably quicker than any other did. His ears did not get any more erect than normal when I flicked the record button, so in future, the ka-chik of a shutter may not disturb them. Anyway, he jogged diagonally to his right, stopping at the sycamores, as if scent marking them, and gave me a thoroughly good staring, giving me an excellent look at his broad, handsome mask. His left foot was raised, as if ready for any excuse to bolt back down, but all seemed well, and he plodded on forwards casually, stopping from time to time to either gaze at me, or to sniff for potential shoots/grubs on the trodden footpath. (The badgers probably used this more than pedestrians did!)

Soon after it wandered off, the same badger reappeared again, this time from the fence. That as odd – I had just seen it go the other way It followed a path, slowly making its way towards me, only for me to lose sight of it. A rustle to the left soon verified my confusion, as it trotted so close to my right – about three metres! As much excitement as I was in, I quickly came to the fact that it would without a doubt smell me, so I held my breath. Much to my surprise, it carried on carelessly, across the path's "tributary", and into the shrubbery, where I saw the last of it.

With sunset happening in a few minutes, and the sighting of four different badgers, I did not expect to see any more activity for the evening. Nevertheless, just as I said that, the iconic boar came right out of the entrance with the huge spoil heap, trotted through the dry leaves, and across the path. It sniffed at the beech for a couple of seconds, gracefully easing its way through the new shoots behind me, probably to forage with the others. I ended the evening there.

5th – 8th May

As much as I would like to waffle on about these next four badger watches, I would like to keep these shorter, since, all of them combined, will take up too much space. Therefore, these entries will be placed into one significant piece of text. Anyway, after hearing my success on my last two evenings, my brother Magnus longed to come, so I very willingly walked him there that day.

I was slightly concerned, owing to the blusterous wind, that only a couple of stalwarts would emerge here and there. Throwing leaves into the air soon indicated that the air's direction was about south – east, so the strong wind was likely to be a warm one according to the badgers. As I had thought, the badgers came out about 20 minutes later than expected, but when one did (still at day mind you) it gave us an excellent view from less than three metres from where we sat! I had taken it for the cub, but I realised that its hide was perfection, with no tufts, leading to a slim face.

That moment was shattered, when she galloped of at incredible pace towards the sett. Once right out of the sett, they seem rather careless of its surroundings, so this precarious sow must have more acquired senses. We were lucky that this one emerged before sunset, as the wood went quiet as it darkened. Time flew, as no more badgers came out, and we were both thinking how long it would be until we got off the log. As if by magic, the wind dropped, and a face appeared from the depression in the large spoil heap close in front. It had a sniff, and to our delight, was greeted by another badger that had obviously come out from one of the railway entrances. They stuck around, unfortunately with no cubs, and eventually wandered off, ending the evening on a high note.

My youngest brother William too, liked the idea of proper badger watching, so I happily decided to take him, and my Mum, on a warm, breezy night. I was excited, as well as nervous, because neither of the two had seen a badger in the wild, so I really wanted them to come out. Before reaching the log, we passed a couple of men smoking marijuana, but luckily, they had come from another track apart from the setts. Upon sitting down, a woman and her boy came trundling along, right on the footpath, still downwind, but dangerously noisy. I took it that the badgers would think the racket was just a passing deer, and I hoped that was all.

Funnily enough, they came out a few minutes after the pedestrians walked by, which was lucky! The cub used the same entrance as last night and pootled around, as it usually would, before slowly going in. My spectators next to me were very satisfied with their first sighting, and my hopes were raised considerably from what they were those few minutes ago.

Somewhere, on the railway bank, something stirred, and shuffled out of sight, before the boar crawled out of hiding and moved casually towards the rustle of leaves.

There! Whispered William and we all caught sight of the outline of a shape – a cub! Two of them darted about over the torn up fence, here one second and there the next, obliterating any plant in their way, knocking over hazels, and hustled themselves out of our sight. We were eager to see more, but they refused to come to our side of the fence. I hope they had gone somewhere else, because three dogs, each the size of a deer ran to us, barking the pigeons out of the trees. We had to leave it there, since badgers will not like this disruption one bit.

The badgers came out at five to eight the next night, out of the beech entrance (the one with the large spoil heap). I expected them to do what they normally would – go back in, then reappear, but this time, the boar and the sow emerged cautiously for the second time, only with a cub at their heels! This one, I had not seen, for the others had much darker hides, with this one having almost erythristic hair, with a not so striking muzzle.

I assumed it had not come out before, since it was very wary of the surroundings, and it did not venture more than a few yards from the adults. My brother had never seen a cub this close before, when it came pootling towards the peanuts I had put out, and to be honest neither had I! While this bright silver shape (whom I had named Silvia) pootled around slowly in the bits of vegetation, her siblings, or, presumably cousins could be heard thrashing around as they did, the night before.

Silvia soon retreated down with Eilean (the sow's new name), leaving the boar to forage; he wandered down the track to our left out of our sight. He was followed by the female, who emerged quickly afterwards and slowly made her way up the same track, in the male's footsteps. I was beginning to think that these were the only five badgers living here – two adults and three cubs, and I was wandering if the small sow was just the yearling at a different angle. But as if by magic, his jagged coat brushed some soil aside, as he inhaled the cool, evening air.

This sighting meant a lot. If there were three badgers free to forage, then there is more than one family inhabiting the tunnels below us. If the grown – ups had any sense, they would not at all let their young play by the railway track, so one had to be supervising the little tykes on the other side of the fence. Not to forget Silvia, who would likely have somebody down there with her but my theory has not been proven yet.

After meeting up with friends in the woods, Tom agreed to come with me tonight. He, like me does wildlife photography, so we thought it would be a great opportunity to do so. We arrived in the woods at the usual time, and much to his surprise, saw Roman (the boar with the roman nose) emerge at the correct time I had expected, very much in daylight. He poked his head up, and got a whiff of the world after stepping a few feet, before galloping back down due to Tom's noisy shutter. I had forgotten to tell him, that for starting off, it is never a good idea to shoot them when they are most nervous.

In all, up until 8.45pm we scared the badgers four times, without seeing any cubs, so we thought now would be a good time to head off. But just like all the times before, Roman emerged out of the sandy entrance (the ventilation – like hole) and didn't seem concerned at all. He ventured off to where he had gone earlier, and a flow of relief came over me: for next time, they would still emerge in daylight, perhaps with cubs. Unfortunately, despite Tom's efforts, the photos were out of focus, far from his fault. I however, did manage to get one, before it dived into the sett for a second time.

8th May (previously)

Putting the clock back to around 10 in the morning, my family went to meet, Tom, and his family in the woods. We decided to go to the rope swing, so I led them through the winding tracks, before turning right, down a trodden path snaking along. Now, recently, Mike, who lives slightly off-grid, told me of some twayblades that had sprouted around this area, so when my eyes set on a proud green plant, right where a young child could knock it clean out, I ran towards it.

I blurted out that I had found the orchid, but something did not seem right. The leaves were different,

and it had not the characteristics of the plant I thought it was. In fact, later research showed that I had surprisingly found a greater butterfly orchid, which Mike says has only been here once while he was here (many years). I questioned the greenness to myself, but I soon realised that it was not in bloom, so I would have to wait a while. I walked past it many times, and photographed them as the blooms started to come out, and they are still not mature yet.

I will let the reader know when they are in full bloom later on in the book.

15th – 17th May

Tom really enjoyed watching the badgers, despite him and I giving them a scare with noisy shutters. We have learnt our lesson on not photographing the first adult to emerge. Anyhow, he really wanted to come again, so I happily let him. That night included seeing the cubs on an unearthed spoil heap already there as we cautiously arrived, a sow poking her nose up several times and more play. He left his camera out on a tree after walking all over the beech entrance, which made me slightly frustrated, and I shouldn't have expect any more activity for that night.

A day later, he went badger watching with his Dad, and told me all about it over email. A strange feeling came over me, and I sought out what it was. That badger sett is so precious to me, as it is not common for badgers to always emerge in broad daylight just like that. It never occurred to me that this conflict of interest may have broken out. I hadn't realised how much this colony meant to me. I had spent so long looking for a place like this, watching, monitoring clans six miles away, and I reckoned I deserved Mother Nature's gift to me. I was not happy that somebody else had mooched off my hard work, and I felt as if I owned the sett, it was my sett, you had to ask permission to watch it, under my supervision.

I felt so protective of it, and I was terrified that somebody might disrupt it so badly, that the badgers there would only come out in the late hours. Of course, I had not explained this to Tom, since all he had done was get interested, and he may not have had a clue on what watching badgers meant to me here, but I still strangely did not feel comfortable going as he pleases. We were going together to collect his camera from the entrances, in an hour, so I would have a word with him.

Luckily, he had badgers out on the screen a few minutes after we left, and a night later, the cubs were out at the usual time. This gave me some loose slack – they had not been disturbed after all. I had that word with him, and told him never to walk over the spoil heaps, or more importantly, share it with people outside his family. When saying this, I explained how it was our sett (cringing at the thought) so I felt he as contributing to this social group. Luckily, he agreed and I was very satisfied with the result.

I still sent him an email giving him badger watching advice, but also it diverted to what I wanted, like wind, clothing, noise, cameras at the right time etc. It is rather difficult, as I could just tell him all this, but our friendship would likely turn around, though I could get the badgers all to myself, but I stuck with the original plan, and so far, it has worked.

Not only being slightly irritated at those photos, but I was jealous, as I eagerly wanted an opportunity like this, so I went that night. I misheard Tom, as he said he went at 8.15pm, but I thought it 7.15pm, so I went a lot earlier this time, hoping to see some early cubs. The first badger, Roman it was, stuck his head out at a regular time – 8.10pm, and after an hour of waiting, I was thrilled they would be emerging. Unfortunately, though, a deer that was barking a few metres behind me at full throttle delayed the general emergence by 10 minutes. This happened twice. After I threw a stick at the deer, the racket ceased and Roman came out again, this time, with four cubs at his heels.

He went back in, leaving the cubs to muck about, dig, or forage outside the beech entrance. Silvia is the turned her back, and Cotton, the other sow presented a snow – white tail. The four fed in harmony, and seemed quite happy without adults with them Silvia has been more adventurous, as when she was new to upper world a few nights ago, she rarely went away from her mother, and did not stay out for long. Her brother Stubble, a larger boar, shares the same nose with Roman, but I suppose all these cubs did. He seemed to get closer to Cotton than his sister did, often sitting with one another and speaking in chirrups and grunts.

Finally, Cotton's brother is probably the largest of the bunch. He looked bolder, and like Stubble, he foraged further than the two young sows, and I should think he is very protective of his more vulnerable sister. I have named him Hornbeam, as of being naturally hard going, tough – a confident and proud animal.

Four natural beauties are here, all of them perfect, miniature versions of their parents. Hornbeam was the only one who noticed the click of my camera, giving me the thought that his senses were better that the others'. At the time, the light was so poor, so the only option save flash was to slow the shutter speed, but the cubs were not keeping still for long enough. My hopes were in the bin, before Hornbeam got interested. He waddled across the entrance towards me slightly, locking himself in a brilliant pose for a second of an open shutter, so I pressed down. And he did not move an inch!

Mud on a badger's nose always makes me giggle somehow, but I was just thankful I could salvage one good photo from a memorable night.

18th May

Before reading the insightful Leif Bersweden's *'Orchid Hunter'*, I was not particularly interested in this flower species. When I first found the batches of Early Purples, I was intrigued to find out what other plants were in the woods. This I did, and shortly found out that there were twayblades hidden somewhere beside the bracken, close to the junction, where the tracks meet.

My Dad and I were hooked, so we had a thorough search with the whole family, but we found nothing save the usual greenery on the forest floor. It was irritating, but we both recognised Chappett's Copse, where many different orchids bloom, so I was counting on that to give us a successful search, but my Dad was much more determined to find the twayblades, so we searched in the same place.

This was just after Mike had told us that they were gone – dead, nibbled, or dying. This was not convincing news, but we still had a tiresome look for what seemed was not there. I could

see that he too, was not expecting to find the orchids, and that the chances of going home were large, but then something caught my eye. A tall, green plant with snake – headed sepals spewing out of it was only a few yards in front of me; so naturally, I called out to him loudly.

One flower turned to 10, then 20, then 30, then 40! The author of the *Orchid Hunter* once stated, that these plants were like children coming to

play. If you stood still, (which I did) then they would
likely appear into view, if they were there of course.
What was slightly odd is that pretty much all of them
were in great condition; some hadn't even emerged from
their buds yet. This meant that I had found a new set of
twayblades, which will hopefully grow again for next
year.

20th May

        My goodness, I was in for a big surprise that
night. I got to the badger sett at the usual time, only to
find five cubs playing on the spoil heaps! I immediately
recognised the four siblings who were shuffling about on
the right and one more unknown to me with fur in rather
poor condition, probably their cousin. I was still in a
happy shock, but I got to my camera straight away, glad
to see they were still emerging very early. No adult was in
sight, so I decided to follow them around, as they
pootled across the dry leaves with their weak legs. After
photographing the five cubs, Shaggy – Whitetail sniffed

at the beech tree, and wandered off to two more cubs! Seven! The four cubs I recently named must be brothers and sisters, and likewise to Siege, Shaggy – Whitetail, Scrub, who foraged together in groups. I had never been so close to badgers! They came within a yard of where I stood, looked at me countless times, yet turned their noses up at the dark figure looming over them!

Siege definitely came the closest, and I have a video of her ambling next to the tree I was standing. Meanwhile, the other four were chewing on vegetation on the beech sett spoil heap, and I took my favourite photo of Stubble on his own (below). I turned my head back to Siege and her brothers, who

were moving quickly around her as she slowly plodded towards me, so fuzzy, that the photo looked out of focus. I love her eyes, I just knew she was a girl, a sweet, and delicate face with longing, black eyes, with and adorably fluffy coat. I do not like saying the word, 'adorable', but in this case, there is an obvious exception.

I was so interested in these new cubs, that I did not notice three pairs of eyes fall on me from the beech entrance. I froze, and expected them to dash back in, but only one did – the

boar. However, before doing so, he gave the cubs a few licks, for I think he must have acknowledged that the seven other cubs seemed alright. Of course! I had this feeling all along! If you can remember the entry where the cubs first came out, they were quite large and playful. I had not seen them in a while, thinking they had left the territory. I soon thought of appropriate names for them, the larger one, pictured above is Rough, and the smaller one that followed is named Tumble, owing to my first impression of the two. They did not stick around for long, and went off to forage in the field

over the railway tracks, leaving me with the other seven to watch. I got one more photo of Scrub (left), the only one without a snub nose, but these three retired slowly, and seemingly reluctantly down the far east entrance I have not watched yet. The cubs had made my day, but I was slightly concerned about the adult, whom I think was Roman, or Buckthorn (the yearling) – I cannot be sure. For all I know, it could be a different adult whatsoever, as there have to be at least six living here to harvest nine cubs! I slowly crept passed the sett, and the cubs, to sit on the log, in wait for hopefully another badger to emerge.

I turned my camera back on, as the cubs were getting quite close, but just as I did that, Roman poked his nose out of the sandy entrance, watching the cubs frolicking about. He crept towards them and nuzzled them gently, leaving, as he retreated inside the beech entrance. The same thing happened, only with Buckthorn coming out of the same place. It was quite hard to see now, but I could notice his white tail, his perfect nose and dark hide trot off down the path he usually takes. He left the cubs alone, so, like him, I did the same thing.

21st May

After badger watching once, my Dad told me he had found a lesser butterfly orchid off the main footpath, he was walking on. I was excited, so as our grandparents came round for a day, I guided them through the wood to see all the orchid species. My eyes soon set upon a beautiful spike of an unmistakeable flower under a tree, and got down to take photos, ruined by my Grandpa barging in and bending the plant 90 degrees!

The previous day, I had failed to find it, thinking someone had picked or trampled it so I was glad nobody had done just that. I could immediately tell his identification was correct, by looking at the position of the pollenia (which was in an upside – down U position).The petals as well, were just smaller in stature than its larger cousin was, but just as pretty. This was our fourth different orchid in this wood, and before a year ago, I did not really know what significance it had.

Walking down the track, we had a look at the twayblades I had found previously, and then veered off to the left, towards the greater butterfly. This one had taken longer than the lesser to bloom, but it was finally showing all of its flowers. I must say, it was a very handsome plant, easily the largest orchid in the wood, vulnerable to a reckless child. But here it was, here a few days, and gone the next.

24th May

I had not taken my Dad since my first successful night at Downton Grove, (on the 26th April), so he asked me to take him again, which I gladly did. The wind was still, but moving from north to south, so we sat on the log, then moved to a tree stump, where we waited. I was certain that we were downwind, but not too certain. Eilean had emerged previously at ten to eight, but my Dad was annoyingly looking in the other direction as she lumbered back in. She had scented the stiff wind, looking away from us, meaning that there was no way she could smell us. There was still hope.

Anyway, just as we moved to a stump, a huge chocolate coloured dog bounded towards us and made a right ruckus that would terrify the living daylights out of a passing badger. We were both whispering remarks to make the blasted thing push off, but it only lost interest as the owners walked past. What amazed us next, is that the badgers emerged a couple of minute after the racket! Eilean emerged with two cubs, out of the beech entrance, but fear won over her curiosity for the two unwelcomed shapes in her presence, so she dashed back in.

The wind was blowing away from the sett, so we decided to move closer, to our left, so that the beech tree would hide our daunting silhouettes. About 10 minutes went by before two of the same cubs came out of the sett, followed by Eilean. Though was it? No, I had not seen this caring sow before. She had a dark hide, but her rear end was a light crimson, her tail finishing off her interesting colouration. She was in Buckthorn (the yearling) and Roman's way, as the two of them clambered out of the small hole in relativity to its impressive spoil heap. Sandy stuck around, while Buckthorn slyly trotted off, on the path he usually takes, only to be followed by Hornbeam. When he ventured back, his siblings gushed out of the entrance to nuzzle and play with him, leaving Roman to forage. The cubs soon went off with their parents, while others stayed put, near the muddy entrance. Yet another one emerged once or twice, quite subtly, only to go back in, so we quietly made our way out of the wood.

25th May

The shutter on my camera has always proved an obstacle with badger photography, since the quieter video button is not sharp enough to film in low light. I was taking Tom that night, and we agreed to do some photography, so I thought I would bring the pigeon shooting net to reduce the chance of a badger hearing us. Luckily, Tom wanted to shoot video, because his camera sounds like a gun in a quiet wood! I started asking him about raw video, or ways that could sharpen my frames, but it seemed futile, so I thought, I would get away with some cubs.

Before we got out the car, Tom's eye caught on a mute button in MENU, and turned it on. I had been so daft! It was right there in big letters, but I had passed it on completely. As well as feeling slightly stupid, I was also very pleased, as the shutter now sounds like a ladybird hitting the floor. We sat down under the same beech tree as the previous evening, expecting emergence in about half an hour. Rather than five minutes.

The crimson badger tested the air before Tumble, (who she groomed) Stubble and Cotton appeared from behind her and bounced around her as she was concentrating very hard. All

was well though, and she started to look more relaxed with her surroundings, but a yobbish squirrel who tossed and turned himself about, in the trees above startled them all. The cubs stayed put – Tumble tottered off as if he was drunk, and the other two met up with their siblings and Eilean beyond the spoil heaps. I have a feeling that Rough has left, since I have not seen him, but this sett is quite unpredictable.

27th May

After our success on the orchids of Lockley Wood, my Dad and I planned a trip to Chappett's Copse to find the largest colony of Sword-leaved Helleborines in England. When we got there, I was surprised to see how fast we found one. It was right next to the car! We decided to go off – road to the left, and found two clumps of about 20 each, under the beech canopy, (a good start I must say!) as well as looking for potential, rarer hybrids of the Sword-leaved, and the White. Narrow-leaved is a name for them, but it is slightly boring, sword is more of an exciting name for the plant.

As this wood is 95% of this orchid population, it is unsurprising that the colour white was dotted all over the floor, which had to be trodden very carefully over. We came to a clearing, where spikes were about 50cm tall, with flowers that seemed to last forever gaping out. I should think there were about 400 of these plants around

where we stood, among the dappled, sunlit leaves. It was interesting to see how the different plants varied, for some were minute and dying, whereas others, as I have said before, were massive, with petals shooting out from thick, wide, stalks.

I can see where the "sword" came from, because the leaves resemble that of a kind. The stick right out, and are almost sharp in every aspect, mostly horizontal, as you can see in the photo. Some canes stuck out of the ground, and it turned out to mean some hybrids were at the foot of them. Unfortunately, they were not out yet, so we could not see any flowers, but my Dad spotted one a few feet off. I don't know

how the conservationists missed that one, but they must have accidentally forgotten to place the cane down.

There seemed to be a track that led through the orchids, so we followed that, glad to see that there were still plenty about. As we reached the main footpath again, we were met with yet another very large batch, across the verge. Once again, we got down and observed, took photos and felt them, some, like before, were very large and at their best.

Walking on, we found that the woods were thinning out with these flowers, and only from time to time, you would get the occasional White Helleborine here and there. This part had obviously been managed less, since ivy choked the floor, only allowing Arum Lilies and woodruff to live. I did notice however, that there was an enormous badger sett on the northern bank. There were about 30 entrances altogether and 25 had giant spoil heaps, not to mention, that, the nearest and furthest entrances were 60 metres apart!

After having lunch, my Dad spotted a sign for fly orchids, but they were just small shoots, so we bade goodbye to Chappett's Copse, hoping to come another day.

27th May evening

After a long day of trekking about, in the sweltering heat, it's good to look forward to a cool evening of badger watching. Over the phone, Millie and I had looked forward to the night. She had been before in her field, but failed to see one, let alone in daylight, so I had a feeling she would be surprised at the outcome. We sat down on the log accordingly to the slight wind, but I had a feeling that the space wasn't the right one: we were easily downwind, but the wind had been sneaking round to our right, and I was nervous it would eventually lead to the badgers' noses. I hastily told her my thinking, so we shuffled silently to the beech tree. Just our luck though, since the breeze immediately changed, making the log the best position possible.

Millie did a little squeal when the orangey sow (below) emerged from the beech entrance, slightly hiding

her rump, for I couldn't photograph it. She quickly became accustomed to the wood, happily sticking her nostrils into the ground, though from time to time she would look at us and wonder why on earth I was here for the umpteenth time. She came closer and closer still, squinting at us, but she quickly lost interest, and made her way along the ground, to her left. She took the path along the fence, and eventually out of our sight, perhaps to cross the railway line, but who knows? I think I should try following one, to see where it goes. We were having a quiet discussion about Fly agaric mushrooms, when Buckthorn appeared from the beech entrance. He was moving at a quickened pace across the footpath, and my 1/25th shutter speed wasn't fast enough to catch him. It is interesting how slow a badger might seem to a passing stranger, but when the need to run, they really put their feet down. There are records of badgers galloping at the speed of a horse! Only these are not officially confirmed cases. Buckthorn always has the look of suspicion in his black eyes, as if he is up to something naughty, something that is best the others do not know.

I did not really have time to think about this, as Scrub, then Hornbeam, and Stubble came flying out of the same entrance. At first I had mistaken Scrub for an adult, for he is the only cub without a snub nose. They had all grown a little, and Millie quoted on how she just wants to take one home in her pocket! I admit that was the same case for me. I did notice whom I had thought was Eilean' s head bobbing up and down in the beech entrance, but it turned out to be Tumble, who calmly, this time, trotted over the spoil to where rustles and yelps could be heard. I could not see the cubs' parents, so I allowed Millie and myself to edge round for a closer look.

Save Tumble, there were six by the muddy entrances. Scrub, Hornbeam, and Stubble were playing leapfrog, and Shaggy – Whitetail, Cotton were quietly foraging with either

Silvia or Siege. All of them soon reluctantly went away, or back down under, so we left it there, before the light went.

28th May

Tom and I had a bike ride in the morning, and we decided to do some badger photography that evening. Last time had worked really well, so it was a win-win situation if we repeated that. Before sitting down on the log, we noticed some walkers going past the sett, but they were surprisingly quiet, so there was no reason to worry.

There was a noise behind us, and we turned around to see a deer being chased by a dog with bells around its neck! We hoped desperately that it would not come near us, but as you may have guessed, it did. It just so happened that this was when some people started chatting to us, asking about our photography. This would have been nice some other time, as all that I was wishing was that they would go away! However, I really could not, as they were only asking.

Right about the time they would have normally emerged, the owner of the stray dog with bells around its neck, stood about 30 metres behind us and started blowing a dog whistle for heaven's sake! After that, things settled down. Roman soon emerged, and walked down the path where I had scattered badger and fox food all around. He paused to sniff it, but he didn't seem to have an appetite, because he passed it on.

I accidentally had it on Program, and didn't know the shutter speed was on a second, so I failed miserably to get a photo. Tom however, had caught a very sharp video. When I was showing him how my video was not nearly as sharp as his, the sow with the reddish rump and Silvia came right into the frame! I jumped back a bit, but soon to Aperture Priority to try to get some photos. They were getting closer and closer to my food, and

Hornbeam sniffed some of it, nearly in the clearing now. Then something unbelievably annoying happened. Silvia edged backwards, and jumped out of her skin as she bumped into her brother! She and Stubble raced for the sett, and Hornbeam, confused, followed. Tom too was disappointed, and he said – "a train might as well come along now." And unsurprisingly, one did.

Developments

June

28th May – 1st June

I am not sure you know, but I had previously named the badgers in Lockley Wood before I started watching the sett at Downton Grove. My trail cameras were excellent, as in the winter, when it is too cold and too dark to view anything in front of your hand; I left them out so they can monitor the entrances. I got them right down low on the spoil heaps and paths, and kept them there for about three nights on average. I thought that early spring was a great time to do this, as the badgers are becoming more confident in their activity, so this is where I got my thinking.

It worked brilliantly. I got excellent close up views of the animals, and was able to identify all the different ones. I came to know of five adults that inhabited the main sett, but I was sure there might be more in the active subsidiary 100 metres away. Their names were Stubbers, Hawthorn, Bramble, Ol' Doris, and Parvus. They all have small, unique appearances that the cameras showed me, giving them appropriated names, for size, shape, etc. I could only identify them when they would look at me, as a badger's rump doesn't seem to tell me much here.

Stubbers is massive. He is the biggest badger I have ever seen. The name tells us everything – he is a well-built, stubborn, strong soul, unmistakeable to miss when badger watching. When my brother and I first went out together here, we saw a large badger (presumably a boar) emerge before the others. Stubbers' size suggests that he is numerous years old, so it was very likely that that was he.

Hawthorn is a long and sleek sow with an extended nose, often coming out very early, or very late. I thought that she and Parvus were the same badger, but in other photos of her, she had a white seed on the back of her front leg. She is extremely observant, and usually gives every piece of her surroundings a good look before fully emerging, along with a keen sense of smell. I named her Hawthorn, as it seemed the most feminine of the 'thorns', and because of her thorn-like snout.

Bramble is very noticeable, as he has a chewed neck, and a few scars on the left of his muzzle. Sow badgers I have noticed, have conspicuous teats under their bodies, and in cases with Bramble, when his legs are neatly lined, I cannot make out any breasts at all. I know others have made the scars, in a scuffle, but they also give me the impression that he has had a nasty experience with brambles. He is rather similar in size to Parvus, but stockier, and more bulky, owning a small, shaggy tail.

Parvus is Latin for small, as she is certainly the smallest adult in the sett. I often get her mixed up with Bramble, but her face and most of the rest of her is very tidy, and almost perfect, a few tufts here and there on the other hand, ruin her long tail. I think she was once a cub that grew up here, though that is only a presumption, since she could very possibly have come from a neighbouring sett. Close up, she appears lesser compared to the others, but on a wider angle, I would easily mistake her for Hawthorn. Head on, she doesn't look like the slim girl she is, though I soon came to notice that her face curls the nose up into a slight point if placed at the right angle. This stature seems lady-like, and quite apart from most of her in laws, who totter off messily, it looks like she is trying her best to look good in front of the camera!

I was very interested in Ol' Doris, because I just thought she was Hawthorn or Stubbers when I caught a couple of videos of her. I had placed my camera looking at one of the furthest entrances that was being the most used, so I hoped to get footage of potentially a new badger. The only problem was that when I replayed it, I could not get a view of anything underneath her, so when she came into the frame, I could only assume she was another boar, due to her huge size. I moved to the next one, and was surprised that she gave me a nice sight of her flowers! I also noticed that she had a scar on the right of her face, which will be very helpful, for future identification. Her nose had been crinkled with age, and she had large, triangular ears. I was glad there were at least five badgers living here, as this sett has 50+ entrances, and it would be a shame to waste it on a lower number. It felt odd that there was an irregular ratio of males to females, though I knew that these occurrences are not uncommon, for not all the sows give birth.

After using the trail cameras, I started to see earlier emergence, at a consistent time, so I decided to start the season of badger watching. I did not see much while at the sett, so I moved further afield, where I found the group in Downton Grove. Putting them down for a few months (I preferred to see the badgers in the flesh) stopped me from getting any footage for a while, but I began wondering if the cubs had started to properly venture out. Last year, they came late, and I finally caught them after summer solstice, but because of my experience with that one cub under my feet, I thought they would already be emerging.

While I was anointing the sett, I had numerous times seen that the play tree was being used once again, so I thought I had a good chance of capturing something good. I noticed a slanted hazel that looked right at two active entrances and worn down grass with chalk sprinkled all over it. This was promising, so I left it out for four nights.

Four! Last year there were only two! The earliest they would come out was ten past eight – a competitor for the Downton Grove colony? New cubs often emerge in light though, and I thought this was just a one off, but the first badger that tested the air was Hawthorn! She did not stick around, but the cubs definitely did. They simply loved the yogurt bars, oatmeal and badger food, and fed for about two and a half hours! They were not as confident when they first appeared, but when they started, they just could not stop, and I even witnessed some competition, as there would be frequent ear biting and playful tussling.

I have heard some lovely noises made by badgers, like chirruping, grunting, wheezing, whining and more, but I have never heard a low, 'whivelling' noise. They would make this often when having a wrestle, and I am sure it is quite a common vocal for them, yet I had never picked it up before. I could see why the place was so trampled now. I knew all along that it was badgers, but I did not expect them to sit there for these prolonged periods at a time.

They were still very active by 9.35pm, still seemingly with empty stomachs, for the smacking of their chops was louder than ever now. However, they go as quickly as they come. There was loud feeding for another few minutes, but they soon dispersed like pixie dust. I happened to have another camera a few metres away, with scattered peanuts, so I thought they must have gone there to simmer their hunger.

What I really wanted was a caring adult to come in and nuzzle the cubs, so I could get a picture of who was whose parents/young. Unfortunately, though, I did not get any more footage that night, but on the next, my questions were answered. They had come out of another entrance, and came to feed on the food, only this time, with a caring mother. She nosed them and groomed them, and at one point, one of them lent up to kiss her! I did not recognise her, and immediately noticed her short and wide nose, and as of that, I have named her Maple – a leaf that is short and wide. I now know that she is a she, because one of the videos showed that three cubs tried to bowl her over, in an attempt to have a drink! I reckoned she must have been in the subsidiary while I was filming in spring, and moved to the main sett while she was lactating. Most of Maple's activity in front of the camera was only for a couple of minutes, as most of the food had been eaten the night before. I expect she had had enough of this unknown food, and went off where they could find something a little bit more natural.

After a brilliant session, I decided to put one camera out again, for three nights this time in the same place, so I wonder if I'll get anything then.

5th June

As usual, I walked down to Downton Grove on a warm, breezy evening. I obviously wanted to watch and photograph the badgers, but I promised myself to try hard to get a nice frame of either only its head, or a half-hidden portrait. Nearing the longest day of the year, I had expected emergence, a few minutes before sunset, like the first watch here, but then again I did not – I had seen Roman come out an hour and a half before darkness.

I arrived at the regular, 7.30pm, but some walkers was the only action I saw for about an hour. There

seems to be a stage on every watch, where I just think to myself, what am I doing here, when I could be enjoying the comforts of bed? That always, as you might have guessed already, turns around when two of the most boring colours appear – black and white. I was wondering if this was going to be my first blank night, after an almost perfect record, but I then saw Roman (above).

I had my camera trained on the beech entrance, and I was not expecting to see his bulk shift out of the sandy one. He is huge, and his hide is almost bear colour (probably not a pleasant sight for an unaware passer-by), which is funny; for I specifically remember seeing him occasionally in a silver coat. Anyway, he gave me a lovely stare with his lulling black eyes, before calling out to two cubs: Cotton and Stubble. Roman casually wandered down the track to my

left. I visually remember his pose on my first video of him, and he did it again, as if had mirrored time. The cubs have definitely grown, and their snub noses are disappearing, especially Stubble. They played very nicely together, gently tumbling about in the goose grass, while attempting leapfrog at the same time.

I love to see the whole of a badger cub's soul right in its face; full of livelihood and brightness, glad to see that the badgers here still have that life in them.

Later on in that week, I decided to bike up to a sett near my old Primary School to see if it would be easy monitoring it with my trail cameras. I was next to one of the larger spoil heaps, when a badger's face caught my eye. I froze, pondering on what to do next, but there was no need, for the cub (it was) was still, too still. There was no life in it. The face had dulled to a sickly yellow, with no twinkle or smile, and it was among two others. That sighting put me off quite from that neck of the woodland strip. It is common for very young badger cubs to die, in later, dry, months, of starvation or dehydration, so I have a theory related to this. About 250 metres down the road was a flattened badger, likely to be the sow, or in this circumstance, the three cubs' mother, who failed to get food for her starving young. They died at the entrance waiting for her. This is an idea for a widened imagination though, and a more reasonable answer, was that the cubs had been caught up in a fight with two angry boars. May to June is when badgers mate frequently, and where the males get territorial, as well as aggressive. It is rather sad that they get so ferociously behaved, for it puts one of the sett's top priorities down to the bottom with these vulgar and self-centred fights.

Back to my current badger watching: Stubble and Cotton got startled when Roman returned, for they couldn't see where his rustling was coming from, so then came a flurry of hastily shoving each other back down the hole. He didn't seem to mind he had scared them, and sat on the sand for a while before going off again, only to my right. The light was still going very strong for me to wait ten more minutes for Stubble to emerge again. This time though, was only a brief stay, for he immediately ran to the beech entrance, to slink back in, which, I must say, seems a little unnecessary.

The spare time gave me a little time to think about Roman and the potentially new badger. I remember the one I had just seen had a pale battle scar above his rump, and a very long tail with a white tip. The other is silver, but sharing the same nose. I think this Roman's father, but I cannot tell just yet. While thinking this through, Stubble, Cotton, and their other two siblings bumped each other out noisily from the same entrance as before. The two girls were more careful with tussling, as Hornbeam gave Cotton a rather mean shove, sending her head over heels. He obviously felt awful for what he did, because he quickly went to nuzzle and apologise to her. I did not see any more of the cubs for the rest of the time I spent there, but I was very pleased with my camera results, and, as always, willing to go again.

I found the underlying cause of the two similar badgers. The reddish sow does have a neat head, meaning the slickness and curve of it, but head on, she does look very similar to Roman, as there is a narrow groove above her wet nose, that would at first, indicate that her muzzle is hooked. On one of my first badger videos, May 4th, an individual was in the frame and I thought it was very likely it was Roman, but after a few more sightings of her, I noticed she looked very alike to him at first glance. Having a camera has given me so many advantages, most of them being fairly obvious, but having a long lens or binoculars, does help with identification. Hopefully though, if daylight emergence pursues, I shouldn't have a large problem with details.

9th June

Between the five days in which I had not been to the sett as of rain, someone else had. My brother and I sat down on the log, after walking past a recent den 50 yards to the left, to see nothing for an hour and thirty. While scattering peanuts on the path by the beech tree, noticed that sticks were wedged in the sandy entrance, as if a young child had "placed" them there. At first, I was annoyed, but then I remembered reading that badgers occasionally playfully pull sticks in entrances for unknown reasons. Twice had we seen a roe kid bouncing around, though I never knew it would have the curiosity to approach us. It walked forward and stopped, which at this point, one would think – and off he goes, but no. It kept coming, and gave us a sniff at arm's length! I was considering giving it a handful of peanuts, but I had none left as we cautiously watched it trot away. We were seriously considering going home, for no badgers had appeared whatsoever.

When the people came it was nearly the last straw, and I thought that if they asked what they were doing, we would say something deer related and tell them about our sighting. They did not however but my eyes jokily rolled into the back of my head when they did speak. "Watching the badgers are we?" How long had they been watching for? Did they know the rule of the wind? They said they only went occasionally, and had seen half a dozen two nights before, and a couple the next. After bidding goodbye to the very kind couple, they finally came out of the muddy entrances, but on the negative, the wind changed.

We slowly edged our way round to one of the far beech trees to watch there, since all we saw was a cub or two. There was so much movement coming from the hedge to our left, that it seemed as if the shrubbery itself was the one shaking! I really hoped that one would come into the clearing before us, because all Magnus really wanted was to be close to cubs. There! He whispered, as Cotton showed herself from the bushes. I was rather surprised myself on her size, I mean I could very simply pluck her up with two fingers! She was joined by whom I think was Stubble, followed by four others escorted by Eilean, who from 10 feet seems very small for an adult. As if by magic, they did what we both hoped for – all six cubs, Hornbeam, Stubble, Silvia, Cotton, Siege and Scrub foraged so close to us in the clearing. It was now getting too dark to photograph, but anyway, I really wanted to live the moment, that nobody should take for granted. Their chops make lovely sounds when they are eating, just as well as sticking their blunt noses into the ground, escorted by tiny digging claws.

I am aware this doesn't happen frequently but I just can't get rid of the sight of six small, unmistakeable faces peering at us in harmony. In short, I want it to happen again.

I'm always put in a good mood after a good badger watch, but I want the daylight emergence to persist. I have drawn charts referring to the emergence and the light intensity with not a single watch, where I have seen the first adult after sunset. I know it is going towards summer solstice, but the times of appearance keep going up and up. Most of the activity started before eight, though now, half eight to nine o'clock is often the most common. I wander if those people we spoke to are making this happen or maybe the badgers will just naturally fade into pitch darkness.

I am occupied tonight, so I'll put a camera up there, to see how the place is getting on. If it really means the last watching evenings of this sett, I got what I wanted, and I will always remember it as one of my best badger watches.

10th – 14th June

Thank goodness, I was hopelessly wrong. Like I said before I put my cameras up, overlooking the most active entrances and hoped for the best. That being regular emergence times. I was also interested in how these badgers reacted to strong winds and rain, for I hadn't been watching there in that sort of weather. I thought my cameras were rather exposed to pedestrians, so I didn't put out food, for that might attract dogs, whose owners may be inquired to pick the strange rectangular green thing on the floor.

A couple of days later, I collected them to find nothing wrong with their early rising, and if anything, it was improving. 7.50pm is brilliant! That is about an hour's difference from last night's appearance, showing how incorrect I was about concerning the times.

I noticed that most of the badgers that the cameras caught had emerged from the entrance I was filming, so it provided great opportunities to see the different badgers up close. Most of the activity reached its peak at around 3-4am, when seven could be seen on the screen at the same time. I happened to notice some changes in their behaviour, for the cubs seemed very playful with the adults who, again, seemed more joyous, than at emergence. I then remembered that badgers feel most secure before the sun comes up, hence the

more relaxed postures and such.

I see Hornbeam, Silvia and Cotton, but the adult? Have I seen it? No, I do not recall any familiar ears, nose or eyes. Badger watching for prolonged periods, that allowed me to get close to the animals, has opened my eyes to the characters in the sett. I tend to notice the defining features that I mentioned before, so that I know for sure whether or not there is a new face. This is one of those instances. Because the camera shows the videos from back to front, I only then saw the previous one. I thought it was surely the badger I had just seen, but the tail was

47

like a tack, as well as its head, which was also very thin.
(Later going through told me that she was Eilean) It was
just at the time when I was thinking it over, that
something else caught my eye. There were two other
adults in the frame, a sow (the cubs tried to suckle her),
and this badger. He seemed very affectionate to whom I
assumed his mate, nuzzling her, and licking her hide,
while actually paying attention to the cubs who were
being right nuisances. The unmistakable thing about him,
was that his head was scarred, and his ears had crumpled
into a 'cabbage effect.'

This was when I saw the two new badgers the
most, before dawn, giving me a valid excuse for not
seeing them while sitting out. It seems funny to think
that when I first watched here, I assumed there were
only three!

I was very pleased with the early emergence, so I
put my cameras out again, this time, facing into the same
entrance, rather than from behind it, putting a handful of
peanuts down to where I wanted them to be. I don't see
anything wrong with occasionally putting out food for,
especially in these dry summer months, for when food is
scarce, this could actually help cubs and the starving. I
put them out instead of watching, because it was my
Mum's birthday, and we were having a party with some
village friends.

On the first night, there was movement at
8.45pm, but I only got pleasing footage 10 minutes later.
The litter of four emerged, and almost immediately,

Hornbeam and Stubble got into a scrap. Before they did so, they scent marked each other, something I had not seen badgers do before. While putting their rumps together (above), their subcaudal glands emit a musky smell, showing dominance over the other before fighting. It did, and it as amusing to see each of them roll head over heels in the mud, cuffing the other in what looked like excitement. Silvia bravely charged in, and broke it all up, before an Eilean and Rough, who seemed to have come back, rushed to the scene.

  After that kafuffle, the peanuts were hoovered up nicely, six of the younger litters and the adult snuffled in the dirt to get their share. The only thing that concerned me was Shaggy – Whitetail, for all of the cubs were there save him. I've heard that weaker, poorly kept youths can perish in the scarce and lean summer months. Hopefully, he has just had an extensive groom, enabling him to blend in with the others, but if he has passed away, then I hope it was a peaceful farewell.

  For that night, feeding went on until past nine o'clock, before they dispersed as usual. I do wonder where they go, and often think about finding two black and white faces nuzzling five or six smaller ones in a barley field. The infrared lens cannot point out the colours, coming to me that the adult in the frame could be the sow with the orange rump. I thought back to previous watches, and remembered that with Tom, when we first sat by the large beech tree, that sow who came emerged, after the yobbish squirrel, was part ginger, with a conspicuous white tip on her tail. To everyone else, they have said frequently, that the badgers look all the same. It is quite nice that after weeks watching them, I have started seeing difference in character and appearance that don't appeal to others. These however, have mostly been naked eye viewings, and as shown, in this entry and the previous one, I can find new individuals.

15th June

  Apparently, the orchids at Noar Hill hadn't flowered yet, as of the warm weather, so my Dad and I planned a trip to the

Broughton Nature reserve. Here, there were, Chalk fragrant, Pyramidal, and Common spotted orchids, all of which I had not seen before. A straight track that eased

up the neighbouring woodland slope lead us to the gate of a wildflower meadow. Entering, I was shocked to see how quickly I found my first two species, a blur of brilliant colours that shot out of the parched ditch.

As local as it is, the Common Spotted (above) is a very attractive plant unmistakable, with the streaks of purple dashed against cloudy white. Almost all the spikes (triple figures there were) were in full flower, or close to it. The tallest, and perhaps the most healthy of the species, were on the edge of some form of shelter, gaining a balance of their daily needs, and others, on the top of the flat ridge, despite being pounded by the sun's heat, seemed to be doing just fine. My first impression from the Chalk Fragrant (below), was that it had dumpy petals, that rolled in a deep magenta, but it surprised me to see that they came in all sorts of other forms. Some were the colours I had expected it to be, whereas others were either bright pink, or stark white. What was quite strange though, was that large clumps of these were completely different colours altogether, looking like

completely different species. Some were embedded in grass, and proved a difficult task of photographing them, but most weren't, but for an annoying reason. I saw a handsome spike, and

an area with no other orchids surrounding it. I hadn't really
given it much thought on why there was nothing growing out of
it, before red ants were crawling up my shoulders.

My Dad had become interested his plant identification
quite recently, ashamed on how he wasn't familiar with certain
plants and trees. He had kept a collection of photos of the things
he couldn't recognise, and adding to it, he did just that, and like
me, eagerly got down to photograph the flowers. It was when I
was looking at some fragrants by some scrub, when I noticed the
third species for the day.

The Pyramidal orchid has been named almost perfectly,
as the flowers are very much in the shape of the pyramid. I did
like the dark colour of the petals, other photos had told me
differently – light pink. These ones didn't come in masses
though, and I think there can't have been more than 20, but on
the other hand, I suppose I take these things for granted, for I
haven't had an unsuccessful hunt. I find it interesting how these
orchids, along with the others, will take any suitable space: the
surrounding farmland was very well managed, yet the tiniest
available space, the nature reserve in this case, is teeming with
these small spikes.

This is happening
on roadside verges, where
they are being pushed
dangerously close to
swarming traffic, often on
grassy laybys and the like.
We learned that on the
way back, as well as news
articles, for on numerous
roundabouts, there were
tens of Pyramidal spikes peeping out of the meadow grass! It is
rather nice finding new orchids, and I will look forward to
finding some new ones.

June 15th evening

I hadn't seen the Downton Grove badgers in the flesh for a few days, and I was very happy to be dropped off outside the wood for an evening's watch. There were no peanuts left in the snack cupboard, but that didn't matter so much, I couldn't hope for anything more than the sighting of a badger at its sett. I expected emergence at around half past, about an hour before sunset, as that was the average time on the cameras, a good opportunity for lowlight photography.

I am becoming quite picky on the slightest grain, so I wanted to reduce the ISO, in order to stop it. For a change, I decided to shoot in Manual, as other times in Aperture Priority, the exposure has been longer than a second, much too lengthy for a sharp image. I was lucky to see Roman emerge from the Beech entrance, at pretty much the exact time I had expected. He noticed that the tree where I was sitting had a slightly darker variation

towards the bottom, but no hunch was followed, and he padded over the spoil. His handsome shape stood out nicely against the brambles and weed of the railway fence, as he weaved through there, a few metres to my left.

All seemed well, and he casually walked back to the entrance. What happened then surprised me. He called down the tunnel, to a badger who looked identical to him, sharing the same hair colour, both with a blunt, roman nose. I was going over in my head, how it was if they were trying to irritate me, because I must have seen this badger countless times, and mistaken it, for the individual who seemed unmistakeable. Luckily, my 215mm lens showed me that half of his sight was gone, showing that he was the badger I had filmed a few days ago.

I try to make the centre point of my photos the eyes, as I have done here with the right eye, which is glistening with some of the last light of the day. It was likely this badger lost it in a scrap, but other occurrences including sharp metal, or courageous birds would not surprise me. The two of them trotted gracefully, side by side to the hedge on the left, much as if 'Pirate' (my Aunt named him that) was being shown around. This was repeated three times over the course of about twenty minutes, just as if he was given a tour of the main sett, by his lookalike friend, or possibly a sibling.

Pirate sat scratching his stomach, on the gigantic spoil heap, only he was looking away, into the wind. I made a popping

noise with my tongue against my cheek, to get his
attention, for a badger, though nervous, is very curious.
It was helpful that I could sex it there and then, for as it
sat right up I could not see any teats visible, but a certain
'tip' caught my attention from time to time. I thought he
might just be at the main sett temporarily, but the next
night I went, he confidently appeared at the heels of four
cubs, as if he knew the place like the back of his hand.

June 22nd

I had been thinking about the past sessions at the
sett and as much as I loved that moment when
Buckthorn or Roman made a subtle appearance, I
wanted to witness it up close. I had already planned
where I was going to sit, for I had kept an eye on the
wind for the whole day, as I always do. When Magnus
and I got there, I decided to take the chance. The tree we
perched ourselves down by was within 10 feet of the
beech entrance, so the wind was everything.

I was so careful, testing it with leaves and loose
soil every minute, for I desperately wanted the night to
be successful. The very kind couple we saw on the ninth,
spotted us and whispered hello, asking us if this as our
new watching position. I found it comforting that they
noticed how we shared the same interest, and were
generally intrigued about the badgers here. After saying
goodbye, two teens came along with their dogs who
hoovered up a couple of peanuts. The girl was startled
when she saw us, shocked; she shouted a torrent of
swearing, and Magnus later told me how he was tempted
to do a clown face!

With the wind still in our favour, and us being
well camouflaged (as the girl discovered herself), I felt
confident that they would emerge, despite the
interruptions. I now tend to pass these things on, as I
will still, for a cub's face came into view. It kept going in
and out, mostly out of sight, but I knew that it was just

under the entrance, carefully testing the wind to my surprise. When Silvia (it was) came into full view, on the ridge of the spoil heap, it was a wonderful sight: one of my favourite natural wonders Mother Nature has created. I was just so excited, that I had hardly touched my camera, before Cotton slowly slipped out, then to a dash, racing towards the peanuts. It wasn't long before an adult emerged. Eilean gingerly stepped out, ready for a chance to bolt, and wasn't sure about us at all. I really wanted to get a photo of her, but she was too suspicious, having a thorough think about if it was worth having a forage. Gracefully stepping out, she turned the moment into magic.

She is such a beautiful creature, and it made me so happy to watch her at six feet, on her own terms, smacking her lips in satisfaction. It was so rewarding to see her relax after a short period of tense staring, and although she was naturally nervous, she grew more confident for she started to realise that the strange blobs next to her home weren't doing any harm. I was at first sceptical that herself and the sow with the red rump were the same badgers, for their noses were almost identical, but being so close, I saw that the tails were considerably different, clarifying my doubt.

She was noticeably affectionate to the cubs, and I am starting to wonder if she is one of the lactating sows, for she groomed them and nuzzled them, as well as being with the litter of four on numerous occasions. It honestly surprised me that she was so tolerant of the random food, and the fact that she didn't keep her distance – earlier, a blackbird had landed nearby, and she rushed towards the sett, only to be called back by her excitable young. From time to time, she would give us a hard stare, but that was all, and I was so pleased, she cared less and less. The cubs were having a great time, as they clambered, cuffed and crouched to get at the nuts, shoving the other one to the side to get their share. We were so careful not to laugh out loud, when Silvia jumped on a bent stick, which shot back up, hitting Cotton harshly! She ran back down, but came back after a few seconds.

The feeding continued for about half an hour, where they came closer than five feet, adult and all! Eilean trotted off

calmly to my left, and we eventually lost sight of her
behind the railway bank, followed by Silvia and Cotton.
They were met by four other cubs that comically
emerged one by one from the muddy entrances, that lead
to wonderful play. It was just as I turned my eyes back to
the Beech entrance, when a badger I had only seen on
the camera emerged – the large boar with the cabbage
ears. I didn't expect to see him in this light, for he
seemed to be one of the later risers, but there he was,
right in front of us. He had definitely been in a scrap or
two, for his neck was severely chewed, with scratch
marks on a lot of his stocky body.

He is an unmistakeably individual of the clan, for
his head was almost circular, thinning out to a sleek
snout. He didn't mind us that much, and slowly shuffled
over the heap in such a badger-like way, greeting some of
the cubs nicely. Still eagerly watching the strong,
confident play, for a few seconds, kept me from noticing
another head from the same entrance. The silver boar
with the roman nose crept out, staring at us in
bewilderment. He sniffed, and all of a sudden, I realised
that I had been so fixated on the badgers around us, that
I hadn't checked the wind, so I watched breathlessly,
hoping for the best. Fortunately, nothing made him bolt,
and he sucked up a few peanuts, as a light snack before
breakfast.

After he joined the others, I knew that it would
be getting dark soon. Before the light turned to shadow
though, yet another badger emerged, very unsure of us. I
could make out a slightly ginger rump, and I then needed
no time to identify her. I have named her Freya, for a
good friend in my old class with the same coloured hair,
is called that. She could see that the others were having a
great time, and it was rather obvious that she wanted to
join them, but she didn't like us at all. When she started
walking, I was thankful, but her slow pace quickened
into a run, before galloping into one of the muddy
entrances. Now seemed a good time to leave, as the ten+
badgers were out of sight, however, I wanted to see

Freya come out content. She eventually did, for the cubs tugging on the bottom of her hide persuaded her.

The night was fantastic, entrancing and just lovely. I was utmost grateful that I had taken the chance to sit, and get wonderfully close to them. It is funny to think that at previous setts a couple of years ago, it was regular not to see anything

closer than 30 feet, or not at all. Being persistent and patient is very important – even years of almost nothing will eventually pay off, as I have found with this rewarding colony.

As well as not wanting to severely disrupt the badgers with my shutter (they will notice at this close range), I just thought using technology there and then would shatter the moment. It has been the best badger watch I have been on, and as always – why shouldn't it happen again?

June 26th

As well as being quite busy with lessons with other friends for some hours, and the prolonged stormy weather, I hadn't gone to see the badgers. (It is like I am being left out, now that I go so often – genuine school days, and I would be lucky to go a few times per month.) When one of my greatest friends from my old house in Wimbledon came over for a 'sleepover,' we realised we had some time to kill before nodding off in the tent.

It didn't take a genius to figure out where Stanley, William, Magnus and I were at eight o'clock. Arriving there, I stopped dead in my tracks, when I saw one of the younger cubs making its way through the leaf litter. Backing off toward the sett, it did not seem to sense a problem, and we kept walking. I had planned to go just with Stan, and my previous watching position would be that tree very close to the sett, only its girth wouldn't have the diameter to shelter us from sight. The large beech seemed appropriate, for the fact that Stanley hadn't ever seen a live badger didn't seem to matter to him, whatever the distance. A few minutes in, and William, being the youngest, started to fidget. Seeing him there though, in a massively oversized coat, and his smiley face, stops me from sharply whispering *Quiet!*

Before long, Hornbeam emerged, and ever so slightly moved away from on top of the large spoil. Cabbage (the one with the chewed ears) was up next, snaking out of the small hole, careless of any potential danger. This is probably because of aging – the lack of sensitivity. As helpful as this may sound to a photographer or watcher, the carelessness takes away the chances of it staying still. This is the second time I have seen him in reality, and not once has he posed. Four more cubs thundered out of the same entrance, and met Hornbeam, who ran back for a play.

Eilean followed, and she for a change, didn't mind the wind direction. She went towards Cabbage, and then out of sight. After 10 minutes, the cubs dispersed one by one, and shot down the bank in single file, supposedly towards the two adults. In the silence, William started his fidgeting session again and I really did hope the badgers by the hedge wouldn't take any notice. Tonight had been great, and Stanley enjoyed it, which was all that mattered, but I had a feeling the sett had something else to show us, for it was still very light. My instinct was proven correct, when the back of another adult's head bobbed up and down, testing the wind as it slyly appeared. Her nose wasn't unique in comparison to most of the other individuals, so her coming fully out would be very helpful. When she did, I realised that she was Freya, as an orange bottom came after her. Quite apart from Eilean and Cabbage's reactions, she stiffened right up, erect, unsure if her surroundings would make her feel secure.

Elegantly, she sauntered to her right, freezing to look at us in short spurts, squinting deeply with her dashing black eyes. I was saying before, that mostly, the nervous badger is the best opportunity for photographs, as they rudely stare the longest. Freya was doing just that, but then William did something that made me sit as compact as a statue. He waved at her. Expecting the irritating bolt, I closed my eyes, unable to look. To my amazement, she didn't move an inch! And at times like these, when I recall the events, I do think William shared a moment with that badger. In astonishment, I shakily asked him why he did that, and he came up with such a sweet answer: "I was just being friendly".

Before it started to get dark, we caught sight of some play on the muddy banks, including the six of the smaller litter. After a short feed, they dipped under the railway fence, and ambled off for breakfast. Once or twice, either Rough or Tumble took a look at their day, from the beech entrance, but to be honest, I hope it was Shaggy – Whitetail, for it would be comforting to know that he was still with us. After it kept going in and out, I decided it was time to make our move when we failed to see it. I called out, but halfway down the track, a cub spotted us, only to go about its usual business, just like at the start of this rewarding evening.

Darker Nights

July

1st July

My first thoughts on the wind and rain that battered the peaceful countryside were similar to the ones before – enjoy a little warmth, but I just wanted to keep adding to my research. Would the harsh weather keep them in? What would the light look like when they did? Putting trail cameras out I love doing, but I just love the moment when I see one silently emerge too much. I simply can't get enough of it, and I want that moment to happen day after day after day. The showers that abruptly began made me think again, but I just shoved the hunch away, for a little wet never hurt.

I have a continuous habit of checking the wind against the trees as soon as I wake up, and in doing so that day, I was confident that a repeat of the 22nd was possible. Much to my dismay though, the woods

stiffened the direction, and I felt it twirl round in an eddy. The log was the best for the sandy entrance, but for the beech, I knew I could do better. I stood by a young sycamore, that had a brilliant view of the beech entrance, and the wait began. Ten minutes in, and I caught sight of the first of the evening, at 8.15pm! It was difficult to tell, but I recon I saw a cylindrical tail, giving Hornbeam away. It wasn't long before one of his siblings showed up, desiring the scented peanuts that led to an early breakfast.

Because I had planned to sit by the smaller beech tree by that entrance, I had foolishly put the nuts closer to me, without acknowledging the wind direction. This resulted in the two cubs facing the other way, annoyingly, so I hoped for a less bold adult. Freya soon appeared, but wasn't attracted to the incense of the salty delights by her feet. The cloud cover was intense, so there wasn't much light as usual, and Freya was quickening her pace. My slow shutter speed was not the one desired, so I had to act very quickly, for she had only looked at me once. I did in the end, though another shower put the badgers off, irritating as it was though, I now know that they are keen when the ground is wet, but they aren't fond of rain.

3rd July

Millie and I had been in touch quite frequently lately, and I had visited her fields for the young roe that was rather tolerant of humans, and a badger sett they had found around a month

ago. Unfortunately, the kid wasn't there, however later on, while checking out a sett in a public wood a few hundred metres away from the Downton Grove, managed to photograph a buck. Now, for a smallish, electronic, digital compact camera, I really do have to appreciate how mighty the lens is, for, I don't need length for the badgers (I provide that by getting close), but by putting the ISO to the minimum 80, then I can double the size, giving me about 400mm. The deer, if you were interested, was about 320 feet away.

After finding the gargantuan sett at hers, we arranged another viewing, and we perched ourselves by that beech, three metres away from the huge spoil heap. I really wanted Millie to see them emerge like they did with Magnus, for it would be considerably better than her first time. The time was ticking slowly past the half-eight marker, but they had eluded us so far, and by ten to, the latest time I've been aware of, nothing.

I kept having these hallucinations, where I would genuinely see a head appear, but there wasn't anything there, even though there definitely was. We went past nine o'clock when Cabbage came out at last, but he gave the peanuts a dirty look and just trotted off. No cubs appeared, and our legs had gone dead, so we trotted off as well. At the start, I would feel nervous, for what if this was the only thing we saw for the next watches, but why should I, for every time I think this, I am proved wrong.

6th – 7th July

Disappointed that we didn't see any action from the cubs, I put a camera out, that was eye level to some worn ground next to the muddy entrances. The weather wasn't pleasing, but I wanted to get further evidence of their reactions to conditions such as showery winds, so didn't hesitate on the subject. I also wanted to get a video of the more elusive inhabitants that only reveal themselves in the early hours, for I was sure there was at least one more individual that had evaded me. Because I view the recordings backwards, the first footage I came to was a cub snuffling around just after the break of day. From that evening when the cubs were walking right next to me, I remembered that the one I named Scrub had a large, neat, napkin like tail, that acted as a sweeping brush, as if he was scrubbing soapy water off the compact mud, like he seems to be doing here.

I realise now, that I actually have the footage of this other badger, who I realise now, is a boar, with small, squinting eyes, with a neat, smooth neck. In the frame, he is being very loving to Silvia and Cotton, the video involving him cleaning and grooming her lightly, but despite an almost hairless underside, I couldn't see any teats. If this is the litter of four's father, then this a major lead. I understand now, for knowing that the only badger who acted kindly towards those four cubs was Eilean seemed strange to me, so this gave me a more clarified answer. This boar has a messy coat, and the tail doesn't have a huge difference in variation to the main fur. His head alike to Cabbage's, only it is smoother, with circular ears. I christened him Husky.

Catching him again this time in almost complete darkness, gave me the conclusion that he is the one who has a lie in every morning (there always is). This proved an interesting find, that gave me a wider view of the sett, but I secretly hoped for another lactating sow. I knew there was another one out there, for the night of the 11th June, there had been a badger who did not match the appearances of any other. This was my target. The camera screen gave me it in the end. Frond, as of her curly ears was on screen with Siege and Scrub (not Shaggy – Whitetail though), patiently waiting for her cubs to stop running rings around her, so she could go to Cabbage. As his great bear like bulk knocked the camera, he greeted Frond with a nuzzle, then to finally, the bit I had been waiting for, his cubs.

The two adults positioned their rumps together, and what happened next quite surprised me, for they scent marked each other in the same desired place. Staying in that position for five seconds, they followed each other towards the cubs, who were now chewing their tails in the corner or the lens. I caught a couple more videos of Frond, but none were as good as the previous one. Flicking through, I noticed that because of the darker clouds and gusty winds at dusk, the badgers had emerged later. Despite that, they made the most of the short nights, for they finally retired after five o'clock, which is the equivalent of emerging at 7.30pm.

7th July

That day, it was sunny and hot, with a faint, but noticeable breeze. I wondered that if the badgers had had a 'late night,' when they retired later than usual, it would have an effect on their early evening emergence. Unfortunately, the clouds bulged up to a sickening greyish purple, which irritated me a lot, for it is much harder to come out with sharp photographs when the evenings are darker. To my surprise, three cubs were already out, shuffling about in the hedge, making it fairly obvious they had come out of the chalky entrances overlooking the railway tracks.

I desperately wanted to walk up to them, knowing that they are quite tolerant of unknown objects, but I knew the right thing to do was get settled in the correct position first, for the adults may be emerging soon. They were still out and about after I sat down, but they restricted themselves to the confines of the railway bank, and I infrequently saw much action. The cubs went down after ten minutes of waiting, and Downton Grove ceased to make noise, save the songbirds singing goodnight.

What annoyed me, is that throughout the day, the sun was beaming, and the temperature was skyrocketing, but as it grew dimmer, the cloud cover emerged from its hiding. The extra light from the sun is so helpful when your shutter speed is approaching 1/8th or lower, and as of the sunny evenings June brought us, I must have gotten used to that abundant light. To be honest, I have photographed badgers very successfully with a slow shutter such as 1/8th. It is not ideal I completely agree, but you'd be surprised to find that quite a few of my badger photographs have been taken at that speed.

At nine o'clock, Freya timidly emerged from one of the muddy entrances, though it was only a brief sighting, for she trotted off parallel to the tracks in the other direction. She was moving too quickly anyway, but the light she emerged in was undoubtedly poor, another darker night, strange, for the sett.

10th July

It happened again – the sun was high in the sky, beaming its rays out everywhere, but it would shy away as it sank in the sky. I was not that put off, for I noticed that every time the adults would come out later, the next night would be an early one. I got there to find a couple of hairs running around the entrances, bolting as they heard me clumsily step on a dry twig. The wind was being a little tipsy, but I eventually decided to settle down by the large beech, where the wait began.

For half an hour, I kept hearing shuffling to my left on the bank, and I acknowledged that whatever it was, was getting a lot closer. Much to my annoyance though, one of the hare squeezed through the intertwining twigs. Despite that irritation, I still wanted to watch it, so I stiffened up, eyeing it carefully. It seemed fairly comfortable with my presence, though its instincts got the better of it, leading to a dash away.

For the rest of the night, I saw absolutely nothing. Nothing. This sett has spoilt me. My expectations are so high, that I hardly ever get blank nights. I even stayed out a little longer to see if they were just emerging late, but I still got the same outcome as before. At the sett in Lockley Wood, this night would have blended in with many others, common for my early watches. If I am completely honest, I did expect this to happen, for like I said, I have been spoilt here, and my thoughts now are what's one night less than the others?

Coming home was quite pleasant on the other hand, because although the sun reappeared after I left, it

gives off an amazing shine as it sets, turning the sky a rich red. I live on a hill, so whenever sun retreats closer to the south, I can quite easily photograph it from my bedroom, window.

12th – 13th July

I was eager to keep up with the badgers' patterns of emergence, but I was busy on the 12th, so I put out a trail camera. I put it on the ground a few feet away from the beech entrance, positive that the wind would blow the scent right away from the hole. I thought that I might at least capture Cabbage emerging, for numerous times he had done so, and taken the exact same path down to the bank. Lately though, I hadn't seen much emergence from this particular entrance, but I was keen to wait and see.

The first useable footage I came to was Stubble foraging in front of the camera at dawn. I could tell it was him, for he has rounded ears, scars on his neck, ending with a tube - like tail with a whitish tip. His coat was unusually smooth, and wet, but I didn't recall any rain at all, which was odd, for it was unlikely the cubs had a morning dip! Nor did I know of any nearby water source.

For a few hours there wasn't much action but a couple of brief passer-by cubs, though at 10.12pm, Cotton appeared on screen. She is noticeably the smallest of the cubs, easy to point out, for she has a bright white tail in the shape of a firework. Note that her ears are upside - down 'V's, belonging to the top of a very crooked nose. Like Stubble, she came quite close, feeding on something by her feet. I don't remember putting

anything out there the previous afternoon, so I came to the conclusion that she was either grubbing for insects, or snacking on some old peanuts from evenings before.

After Cotton went away, Hornbeam and Stubble started following her, but became increasingly intrigued about the alien object by their home. The photo shows Cotton as the furthest cub to the left, with Hornbeam next to her, and in the top right corner sits Frond. She (their mother) was not so sure about it, for to be fair, in the open, the camera was quite exposed. I didn't see much of the lactating sow, but for Hornbeam and Stubble, it was the opposite. Then both of them put their developing claws, which were surprisingly very long on top of it, and I could hear the heavy use of their nostrils as the cubs tried to figure out what it was.

When I kept scrolling through the footage, I was very disheartened. There were no badgers before 10 o'clock. As upsetting as it was, it explained the later emergence with or without cubs, the blank night that made me realise how spoilt I am. From half eight to nine, I don't mind, but such a leap like 10 must mean they had a scare. In the next week I knew I could have late nights for there were days of seeing others etc. and neither could I collect cameras in the morning or midday. It meant I couldn't keep up with the badgers' behaviour, but I feel they needed a little break. For practically the whole summer, I have come into their lives unwelcome; they have been nervous, unsure, and less bold. If I gave them a bit of breathing space, then their confidence would perhaps grow, proving early emergence. I'll just have to wait and see.

26th July – ongoing

I was starting to become slightly suspicious of my camera lens details, but as far as I knew, it was 215mm at the '50x' mark, and 4.3mm at wide-angle. These numbers were interesting at first, but I did not know their full potential. When I was looking at some extraordinary fisheye lenses over the internet, I came across one that was so extreme, it could see behind it. Looking at the focal length details, I was slightly taken aback that the lens read 4.5mm. This could not be correct, for mine, as wide as it actually was, was surely no match for this new piece of technology. I did some more research, and found out 35mm wise, my lens has a length of 24 – 1200mm.

In finding that out, I immediately acknowledged that despite the considerably lower price, I can double the reach of a huge 600mm one. Knowing this, I now knew that I had just as much chance of photographing birds as anybody else. Boosting my confidence with that small fact, I kept an eye especially out for birds and other small animals of my interest. Camping in Devon brought me to great opportunities that week. The hilltop in which we were situated had a great view of the sickly orange sunset every night. Seagulls in the distance made a lovely

foreground against it, and I went to bed with a panorama of that kind of frame in my mind, fortunate to focus on the bird in flight.

That following morning, I came back from doing the washing up, to hear that a (later identified) female Grey wagtail had been perching comfortably on one of the fence posts outside, close to the breakfast table. My parents said it had been

there for virtually the whole time I had gone, and I was so disappointed at my bad luck. On the other hand though, if it was there for that long, then there was a slight chance it would come back, so the wait began. To my surprise, it arrived a minute in, posing nicely for the camera. I took about 20 shots before it flew off again, but this was my favourite.

The fence post acting as the perch is at a noticeable angle in the photograph, but that was the stature of the real thing. I tried to level it out in one or two shots, but I thought that that outcome was unbalanced.

My friend Monty and I had gone on a very long trek to Micheldever Forest the previous summer, so for fun, we, along with my brother, had a relatively long walk up to Upper Wield. Coming back, I had a look at the bird table hidden in a nearby hedge, expecting the odd blue tit or two. In a split second, out of the corner of my eye, I spotted some, furry variation shoot into the hedge. Very curious, I sat downwind from the scrub, and lay in wait for whatever it was to appear, camera in hand.

Almost immediately, a whiskery face made way to some peanuts somebody had put out. It came from a small, sandy burrow, and I decided that coming to think of it, the inhabitants of the houses across the lane might know well of this rat burrow. More than one darted about, unknowing of my presence. Now normally, a dirty, thieving rat's head would be something I'd like to be seeing through an air gun scope, but these ones were doing nothing. I think it was the satisfaction of seeing a

badger's nose appear that gave me a little soft spot for them. These weren't doing any damage, but just going about their usual selves, so washing any previous thoughts on these rodents, I started to really enjoy watching them coming and going. Unfortunately, Monty and Magnus hadn't heard me call out to them:

"carry on, I'll catch up!" which resulted in me hearing Magnus angrily calling from round the bend, saying they'd been waiting for 20 minutes! After listening to my small encounters, they agreed to watch them for a few minutes.

All this time, I had been attempting to photograph the rats, but with the sun being unpredictable, and shooting into a dark area, it was difficult to get the exposure right. In the end, I managed to get a photo with detail, contrast, and decent light.

My Dad and I wanted to fit in one more orchid search, before most of the flowers turned brown, done for the year. Orchidophiles had been going to a renowned spot called Noar Hill, famous for harbouring 11 different species, especially the rarer musk orchids. These hunters had been finding the colonies of thousands there, so on a Saturday afternoon, we were down there. I don't think I mentioned it, but in early June, we had gone to Downton Grove in search for White Helleborine, and in looking we, also spotted about 90 Birds Nest orchids. This showed us that we could find things that we didn't know were even there, giving us confidence. Much to our surprise, we did not find a thing! Despite our disappointment though, while having lunch, a juvenile wren happily posed for the camera a

metre away from us! It was so pleasant to watch it sing its heart out for a minute, and what's more, my Mum specifically asked me for a photo of this bird, and I was very pleased coming home.

Epilogue

17th August

The day drawing to a halt, Tom and I made our way through a mainly sycamore woodland of contrast and occlusion, the leaves like golden crisps as they absorbed the last sunlight. Eyrie shadows crept through the first line of trees, choking the ground's leaves, dirt, bracken and the turning flowers, as the songbirds bid goodnight to the peaceful harmony.

A partridge spoilt the silence, the chak-chak-chakking echoing through the near darkness, as recognisable as a thunderstorm. The path bent round to the left, now snaking alongside the subtle slope, which highlighted some chalky disturbance further up. I had never seen the badger sett in this uncanny light, for it was hard to make out as the woodland engulfed it. Save the odd twig that crackled menacingly under Tom's feet, or mine, the wait for the badgers was accompanied by an uneasy quietness.

Time slithered by at a snail's pace, and I was having doubts about emergence altogether. I mentioned to Tom how even if it was an empty evening, the peacefulness of the English countryside (in my opinion) made up for it completely. Our eyes had adjusted fairly quickly to what had seemed to be blackness, only it was a mixture of colours, however not so appealing, but noticeable all the same. The evening slowly pressed on when the first badger emerged.

An adult took a while to shuffle its hind quarters out of the hole, before he or she was content with the delicate breeze that passed smoothly from the north. A cub then followed, and was seemingly clumsier than the adult was. Another, who scurried up the chalk heap hastily, sweetly greeted it, receiving a gentle nuzzle in the nose from the other. The two black and white faces ran rings around one another in the now pitch black,

as close as a metre or two. As we left, their minute
scuffling seemed as conspicuous as that partridge.

Conclusion

At the start of this book, I hoped to gain the badgers of Lockley Wood's trust, and that was where I would be, evening after evening, sitting in the entrances for a couple of minutes, hoping that eventually my smell would be associated with nothing in particular. For almost a month, I would repeat the same routine, until I watched the sett at Downton Grove, one that I knew was there, though I was so oblivious to its existence.

The 26th of April changed the entire summer for me. That night, or day, I should call it, opened a wide window of opportunity. I was down the following week, the next day, then the next, and the next. Little by little, I gained information about this other world. Putting camera traps out, it enabled me to enhance my knowledge as I discovered there were not three individual adults, but seven. There were not only four cubs, but nine, excluding the yearling.

At night, debates lashed around my mind as to who were the parents that raised the bunch of rapscallions they put up to live with. Near the start of July, I caught some video footage of all the things I needed to conclude my unrested thoughts. Cabbage, a large bearlike boar, is Frond's, a lactating sow's mate, who had given birth to Siege (sow), Scrub (boar), and Shaggy – Whitetail (boar, who sadly, may not have survived the lean summer). Eilean, who has always shown plenty of affection towards the four siblings, Hornbeam, Stubble, Cotton and Silvia, and in finding that a tall, shaggy badger named Husky, did the same to the cubs and her, my confusion was sealed.

May 20th gave me even more delight, when while watching the cubs, I noticed three faces sitting in the beech entrance. One of them was Roman, while the other two were larger youngsters I had seen with William. Rough and Tumble were almost comparable in size to their mother, Freya. The orange tinted sow had spent time on many occasions grooming the both of them, at the same time showing care to Roman, who I might say, was a little less enthusiastic than the cubs!

My small predictions on the night of the 26th, where I wondered whether there were only three adults, could not be proven more incorrect. I had seen Roman, Eilean, and the yearling, Buckthorn, so unknowing that there were five more, including Pirate, whom I had only seen until very recently.

Many people ask me how I can ever tell the badgers apart, for to them, they all look identical. Since I discovered there were more than three individuals, I would always look for the tiniest features, including, colouration, faces, noses, ears etc. I took the photographs also for pleasure, but mostly for the identification, helping me get a bigger picture of who was who, and who was the same one I had just seen, giving me the satisfying result of 17 individuals! I am very surprised myself, for with the population density being so high in Southern England, the average sett in Hampshire contains 6.5 animals.

Schools look like they will open again in September so I may never have such a long stretch of

time again where I am free from the demands of formal education to go badger watching. At the start of lockdown, I set myself the task of getting within touching range of a badger, who had accepted my scent as nothing dangerous. I realise now, that I do not need that. Superb evenings like May 20th, and 21st June, showed that watching the badgers on their own terms, without knowing I was there, was even better than feeding them. At one, Eilean came within five feet of me, and it made me appreciate the moment even more, for it meant my camouflage was good. She would come closer and closer, cautiously hoovering up the peanuts, relaxing as she felt more comfortable. It was the closest I had been to an adult, and it seemed exactly what I had wanted at the start of it all. Knowing that I pretty much achieved my task, getting within an incredible distance of the badgers, my summer turned out to be a great one. My hard work paid off. The sett had done me brilliantly. It enabled me to watch at a very close proximity, to photograph and appreciate one of Britain's most enigmatic and wonderful animals.

Thomas Gray

For more wildlife images, follow Thomas on
Instagram @downtongrove

www.ingramcontent.com/pod-product-compliance
Lightning Source LLC
Chambersburg PA
CBHW061516250726
48657CB00005B/1901